Why I Live in
MISSISSIPPI

101 Dang Good Reasons

Ellen Patrick

Copyright © 2004 Sweetwater Press

All rights reserved. No part of this book may be reproduced by any means whatsoever, neither mechanical, electronic, nor digital, without written permission from the publisher, except brief excerpts quoted for purpose of review.

ISBN 1-58173-289-9

Jacket and text design by Miles G. Parsons
Compiled with help from Patrick Davidson
Printed in Italy

10 9 8 7 6 5 4 3 2 1

1. Cotton's cheaper.

2. Elvis.

3. Big hair is big business.

4. Strangers still say "Hey!"

―᎒―

5. There's a profit to be made from New Yorkers who think we're quaint.

6. Riverboat gambling.

7. Mud pie.

———

8. Mannings are as abundant as mayonnaise.

9. No syrup, just honey.

—⚡—

10. No oatmeal, just grits.

11. World's best truck stops.

12. It's not West Virginia.

—⚎—

13. The Delta.

14. Cat-head biscuits and sawmill gravy.

15. Boiled peanuts.

16. Anybody else got a town named Hot Coffee?

17. The seventies never went out of style.

18. Beauticians have mayoral status.

—◊—

19. Elvis.

20. Farm-raised catfish.

—⁂—

21. Catfish soufflé.

22. The River.

23. Tomato sandwiches.

―∞―

24. Banana sandwiches.

25. Vicksburg keeping the past alive until time travel becomes more practical.

—⁂—

26. Second helpings encouraged.

27. Your sisters and brothers never move away.

28. Black-eyed peas.

29. The Natchez Trace.

30. The Gulf, God's gift to all (and we're nice enough to share it).

—m—

31. Lax leash laws make for better home security.

32. Side orders of bacon break Guinness records for size and weight.

―∞―

33. More accomplished mockingbirds.

34. Magnolias in spring.

35. Red clay eliminates confusion as to where exactly you are.

36. We're the reason God invented the Blues.

37. Squirrel hunting a nice pastime for the whole family.

---

38. You never see a state trooper.

39. Sweet tea.

40. Others have forests. We have tree farms.

41. Bo Diddley.

—⁓—

42. B. B. King.

43. No worries about potential peroxide shortage.

44. Brakes last longer due to lack of inclines.

—∞—

45. Very little risk of people being too thin.

46. Jimmie Rogers.

47. Elvis.

48. Devil's Punch Bowl.

—⁂—

49. The Singing River.

50. We still eat lunch sitting down.

—∞—

51. We still drink beer standing up.

52. Dinner invitations include the kids.

53. The Mississippi Sandhill Crane.

54. Robert Johnson.

---

55. We eat both dinner and supper.

56. We have two kinds of moonshine.

57. Only state included in the Arabic numeral system (1 Mississippi, 2 Mississippi).

58. Barges.

—∞—

59. Redbuds in spring.

60. The Neshoba County Fair.

―∞―

61. People are so friendly they actually frighten many Yankees.

62. Best corn bread on earth.

---

63. Worst case of football fever on earth.

64. Suits are strictly church wear.

65. Overalls are business casual.

66. Dually-friendly parking spaces.

67. Ole Miss.

—∞—

68. Southern Miss.

—∞—

69. Mississippi State.

70. Everyone is related.

—⚬—

71. Lightning bugs.

72. Moon pies.

73. Elvis.

74. Where else can a blue tick hound sit at the dinner table?

75. No shortage of free advice.

———

76. No inconvenient lines drawn between fact and fiction.

77. Building codes on the creative side.

———ooo———

78. Home of 101 uses for a spare tire.

79. Five 'n' Dimes.

---

80. More church suppers per capita than any other state.

81. Newspapers still cost a quarter.

82. Howlin' Wolf.

—⌇—

83. Muddy Waters.

84. Possum is a nice alternative during beef scares.

85. We still appreciate a nice cold "co-cola."

---

86. Ten bucks still goes a long way.

87. Coconut cake.

—∞—

88. Red velvet cake.

89. Gumbo!

90. We still say our prayers every night.

91. We pray the Yankees don't move South.

---

92. We like Bambi in a special way: medium rare.

93. J. J. Newberry was a national hero.

94. No shortage of corn for eating.

95. No shortage of corn for drinking.

96. No shortage of spare parts for your pickup.

---

97. Christmas decorating is easier when you live in a trailer.

98. Folks will do anything for you (whether you want them to or not).

99. We're the reason God invented partying.

100. We might very well be the reason God invented great literature.

101. You can leave Mississippi, but you'll always come home again.